Weather

Penguin
Random
House

Series Editor Deborah Lock
US Senior Editor Shannon Beatty
Art Director Martin Wilson
Designer Radhika Kapoor
Managing Art Editor Ahlawat Gunjan
Managing Editor Soma B. Chowdhury
DTP Designers Anita Yadav, Vijay Khandwal
Picture Researcher Nishwan Rasool
Producer, Pre-production Francesca Wardell
Jacket Designer Martin Wilson

Reading Consultant
Linda Gambrell, Ph.D.

First American Edition, 2015
Published in the United States by DK Publishing
345 Hudson Street, New York, New York 10014

15 16 17 18 19 10 9 8 7 6 5 4 3 2 1
001—278928—June/15

A catalog record for this book is available
from the Library of Congress.

ISBN: 978-1-4654-3510-1 (Paperback)
ISBN:978-1-4654-3511-8 (Hardcover)

DK books are available at special discounts when purchased in bulk for sales promotions,
premiums, fund-raising, or educational use. For details, contact:
DK Publishing Special Markets
345 Hudson Street, New York, New York 10014
SpecialSales@dk.com

Printed and bound in China

The publisher would like to thank the following for their kind permission to reproduce their photographs:
(Key: a=above, b=below/bottom, c=center, l=left, r=right, t=top)
1 123RF.com: Chee-Onn Leong. **3 Alamy Images:** Peter Phipp/Travelshots.com (br). **4 123RF.com:** Gunnar
Pippel (t); Mazuryk Mykola (b). **5 Corbis:** (b), **iStockphoto.com:** bethsp (t). **6–7 iStockphoto.com:** lypnyk2.
8–9 Alamy Images: Peter Phipp/Travelshots.com. **10–11 123RF.com:** zoomteam. **11 Corbis:** Michael
Thornton/Design Pics (t). **12–13 Getty Images:** PETER STEFFEN/Staff. **14 iStockphoto.com:** SKLA.
15 iStockphoto.com: OGphoto. **16 iStockphoto.com:** ArtShotPhoto. **17 Corbis:** Ariel Skelley/Blend Images.
18–19 123RF.com: Concetta Biddeci. **20–21 Corbis:** Sodapix. **21 Corbis:** Jerry Cooke (tr).
22–23 iStockphoto.com: Juanmonino. **24–25 iStockphoto.com:** andykazie. **25 Corbis:** Solvin Zankl/
Visuals Unlimited (b). **26–27 123RF.com:** Graham Oliver. **28–29 Corbis:** Johan Wouters/Buiten-beeld.
29 Corbis: Barry Lewis (t). **30 123RF.com:** Jerry Horn (cla); lurin (clb), **Corbis:** Solvin Zankl/
Visuals Unlimited (bl), **iStockphoto.com:** ArtShotPhoto (cl); bentrussell (tl).
Jacket images: Front: iStockphoto.com: Imgorthand. **Back: 123RF.com:** Gunnar Pippel t/ (flowers),
Corbis: Jerry Cooke (cr); Solvin Zankl/Visuals Unlimited (cl), **iStockphoto.com:** photo5963 t/ (window).

All other images © Dorling Kindersley
For further information see: www.dkimages.com

A WORLD OF IDEAS
SEE ALL THERE IS TO KNOW

www.dk.com

Contents

Look outside!

sunny

cloudy

4

What's the weather like today?

rainy

snowy

Sun

Today is sunny and hot.
The sun shines brightly.

We have fun
at the beach
on sunny days.

beach

Clouds

Today is cloudy
and warm.
The clouds can be
fluffy or wispy.

Fog

Today is foggy
and damp.
It is hard to see
in the gray fog.

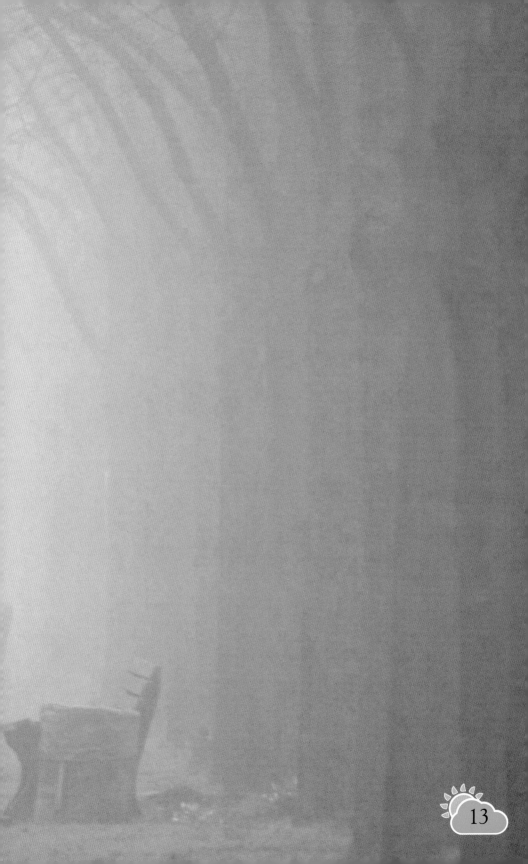

Rain

Today is rainy and wet.
The rain pours down.
Pitter-patter!

raindrop

boots

puddle

We splash in the
puddles on rainy days.
Splash!

Storm

Tonight is stormy.
The lightning flashes
and the thunder booms.
Crack!

lightning

Wind

Today is windy
and cold.
The wind blows
the clothes.

clothes

Gale

Today is very windy
and very rainy.
The trees sway
in the gale.

Snow

Today is snowy
and freezing.
The snow turns
the yard white.

snowflake

gloves

snowman

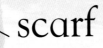

scarf

We wear warm
clothes to play
in the snow.

Rainbow

Look!
The sun shines
through the rain.
It makes a rainbow!

Glossary

Beach
sandy or pebbly
shore by the ocean

Lightning
flash of light
in a storm

Puddle
small pool
of water

Snowman
person-shape
made of snow

Snowflake
small, soft piece of
frozen water (snow)

Index

Have you read these other great books from DK?

LEARNING TO READ

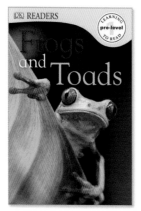

Croak! Move in closer to look at the frogs and toads of the world!

Chatter! Meet the monkeys as they scamper, climb, and jump.

Play and have fun! Enjoy the colorful days throughout the year.

BEGINNING TO READ

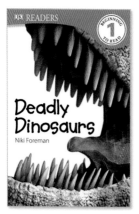

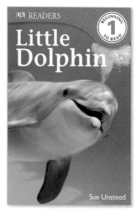

Roar! Thud! Meet the dinosaurs. Who do you think is the deadliest?

Click! Whistle! Join Little Dolphin on his first ocean adventure alone.

Hard hats on! Watch the busy machines build a new school.